Weather, Earth, and Sky

Dona Herweck Rice

spring

summer

winter

autumn

The Tropical Seasons

dry season

wet season

monsoon

The Water Cycle

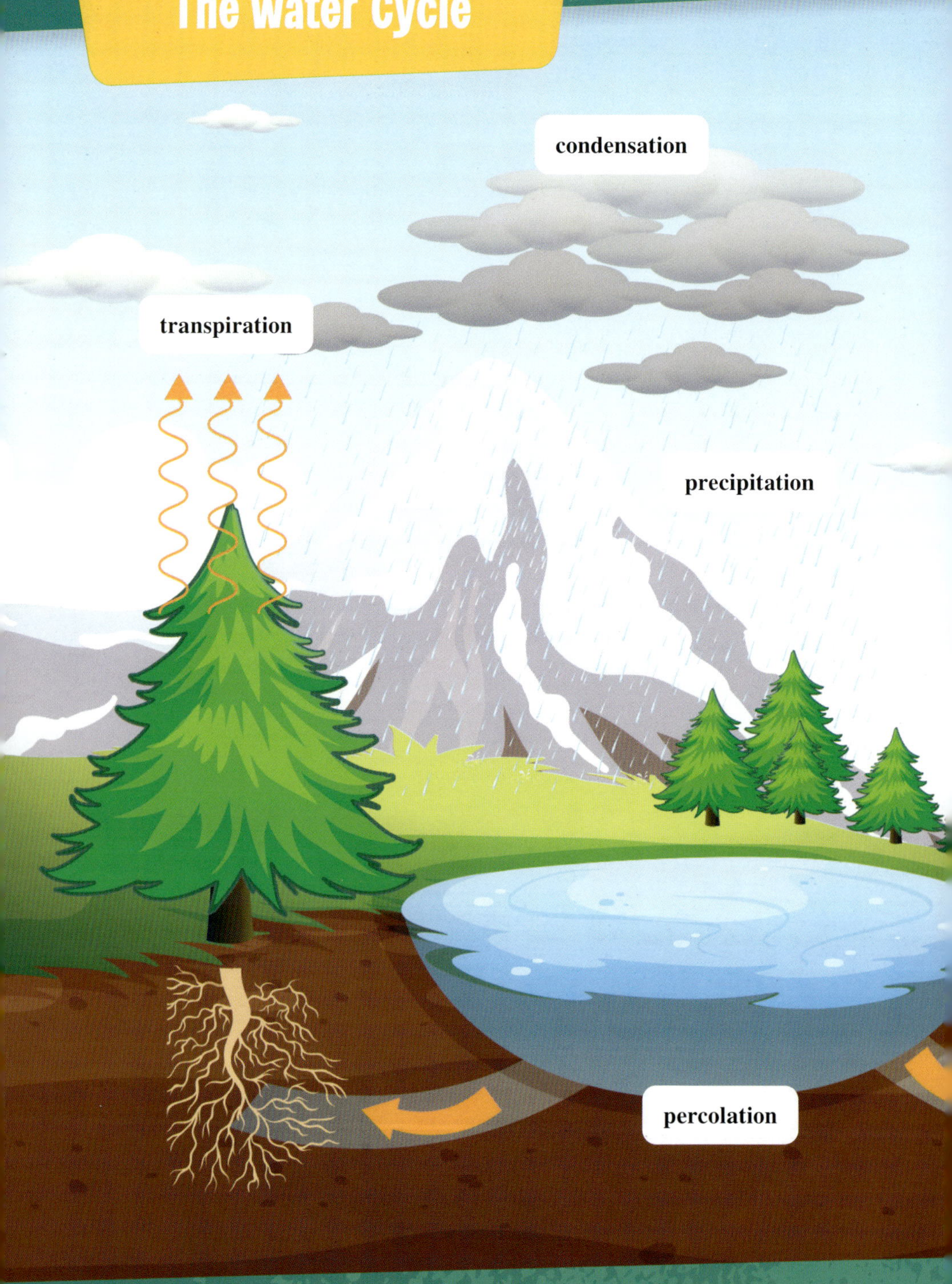

condensation

transpiration

precipitation

percolation

evaporation

low tide

high tide

Earth

high t

low tide

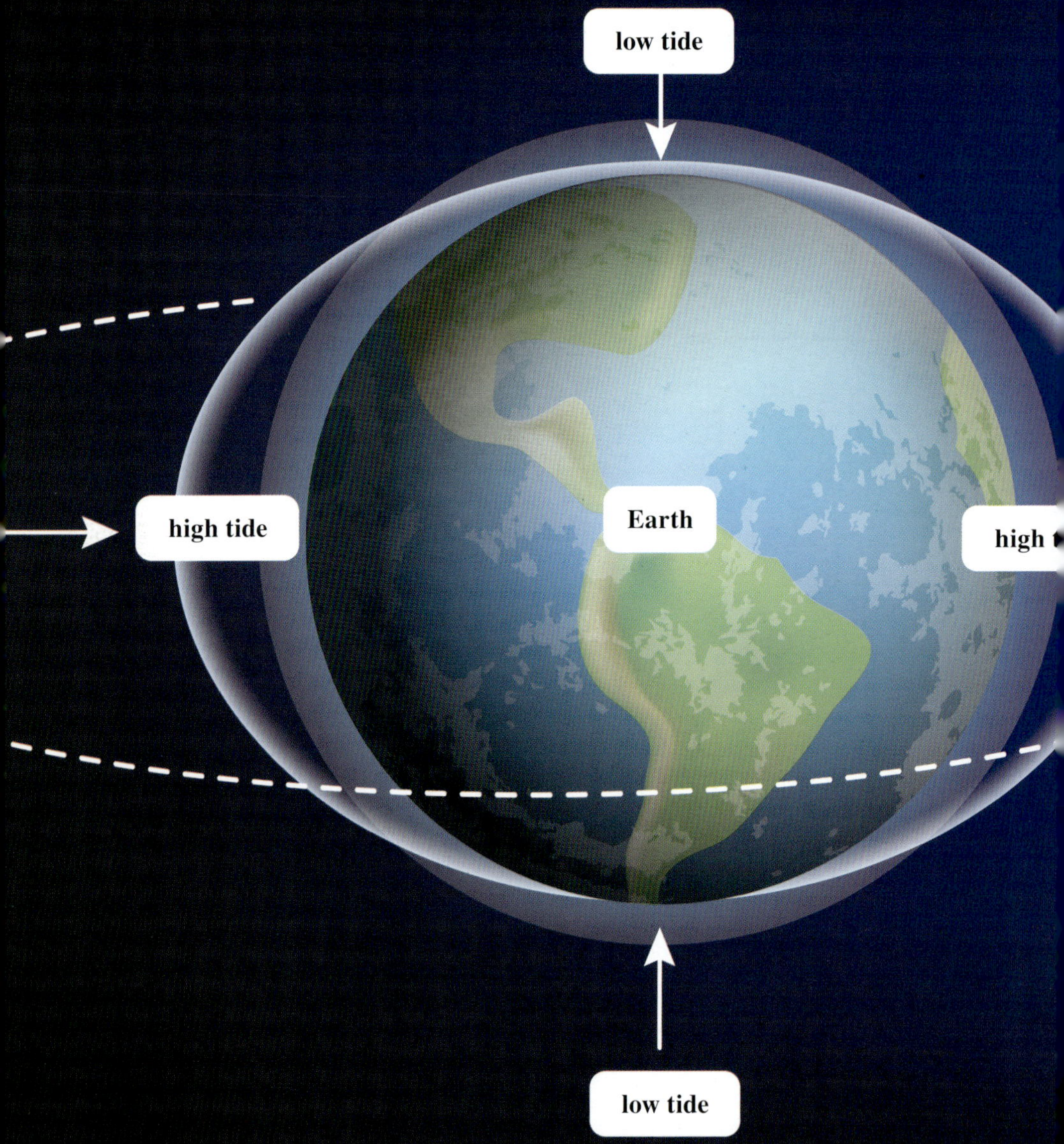

low tide

moon

high tide

Earth's Changing Shorelines

sea

bay

peninsula

Earth's Changing Shorelines

cliffs

sea stacks

coastal bench

sea arch

Earth's Changing Shorelines

estuary

tidal flat

barrier island

lagoon

fjords

Earth's Changing Landforms

mountains

canyon

hills

valley

plateau

prairie

Earth's Changing Landforms

volcano

dunes

glacier

island

swamp

bayou

19

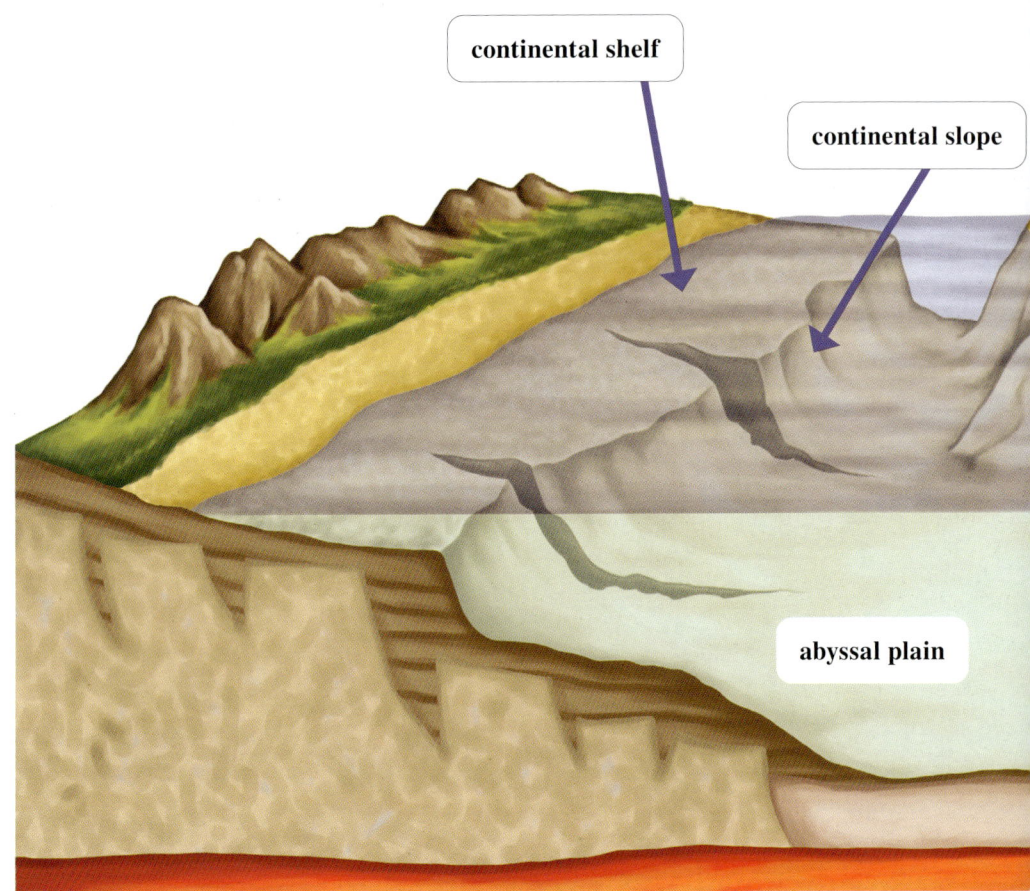

continental shelf

continental slope

abyssal plain

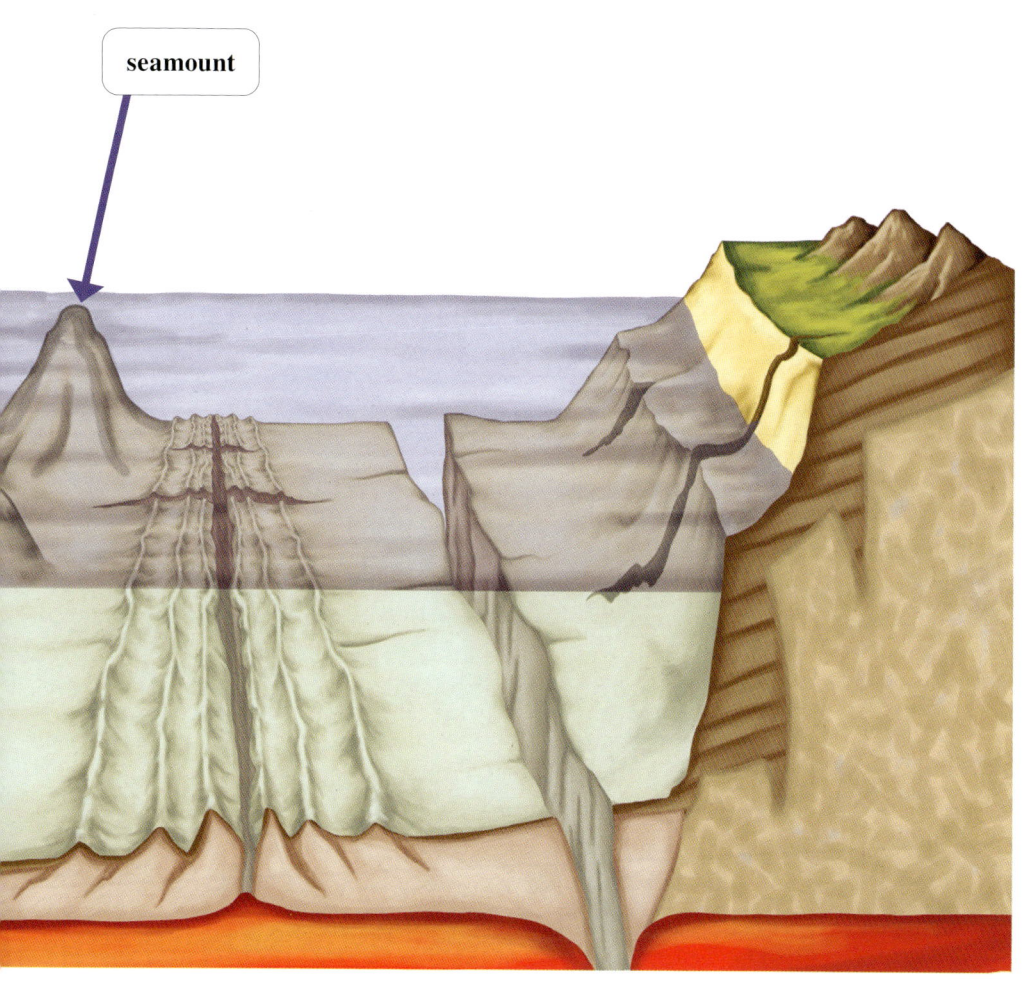

seamount

Earth's Changing Underwater Landforms

volcanic island

ocean basin

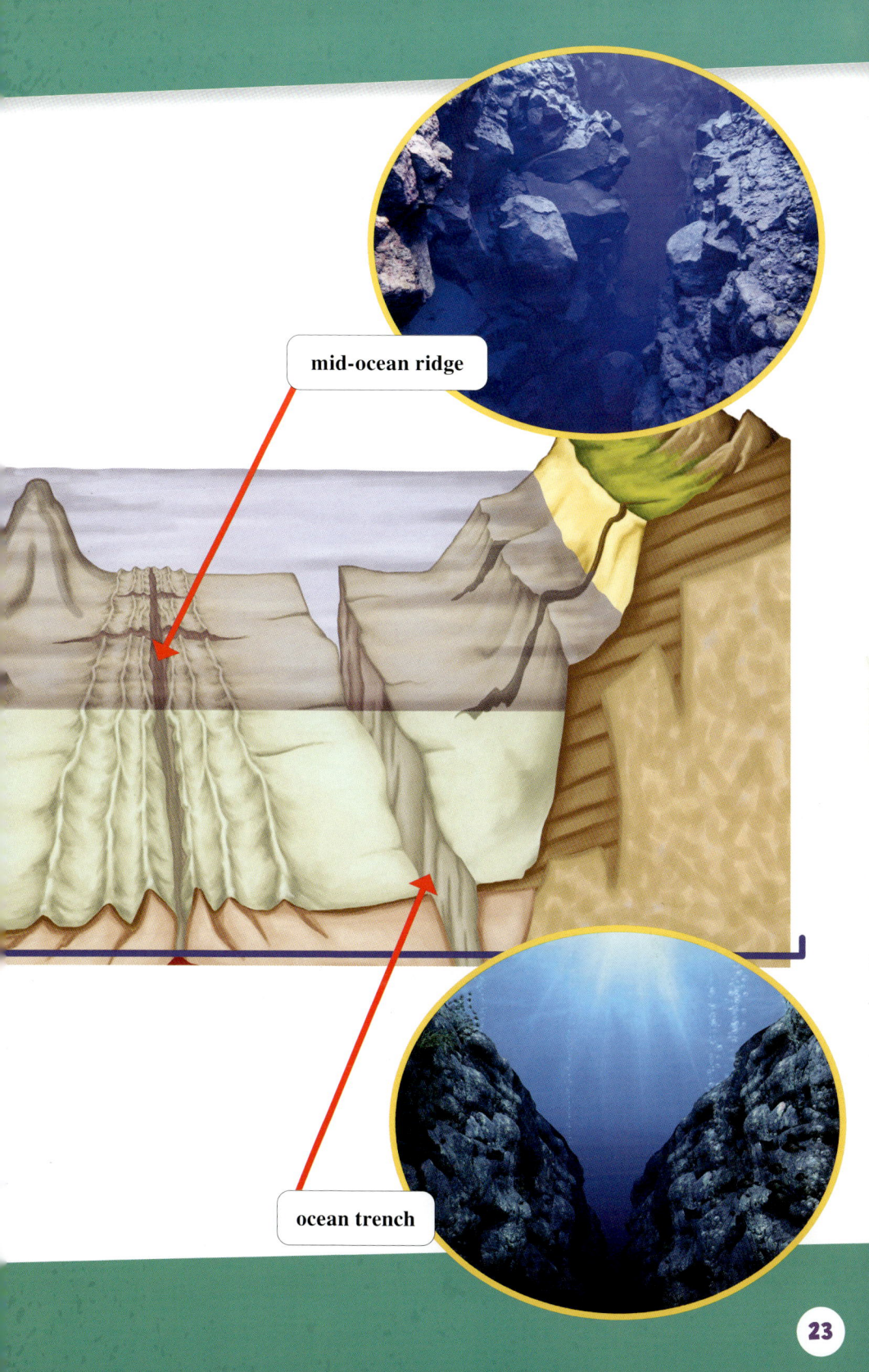

mid-ocean ridge

ocean trench

Change Through Erosion

wind erosion

ice erosion

water erosion

water erosion by waves

water erosion
by flood

transportation

deposition

Change Through Weather

rain

snow

hail

frost

27

heat

drought

lightning

fire

Change Through Movement

landslide

geyser

volcanic eruption

earthquake

Consultant
Cheryl Lane, M.Ed.
Secondary Teacher

Publishing Credits
Rachelle Cracchiolo, M.S.Ed., *Publisher*
Emily R. Smith, M.A.Ed., *SVP of Content Development*
Véronique Bos, *VP of Creative*
Fabiola Sepulveda, *Art Director*

Photo Credits: p.9 Alamy/Laszlo Podor; all other images from iStock, Shutterstock, or in the public domain

Library of Congress Control Number available upon request.

5482 Argosy Avenue
Huntington Beach, CA 92649
www.tcmpub.com
ISBN 979-8-3309-0489-1
© 2025 Teacher Created Materials, Inc.
Printed by: 51497
Printed in: China